Adrian Peterson

by Michael Sandler

Consultant: Norries Wilson
Head Football Coach
Columbia University

New York, New York

Credits

Cover and Title Page, © G. Newman Lowrance/Getty Images, AP Images, and Joseph Sohm/ Visions of America, LLC/Alamy; 4, © AP Images/Jim Mone; 5, © Eric Miller/Reuters/Landov; 6, © K.C. Alfred/Union-Tribune/Getty Images; 7, © Eric Miller/Reuters/Landov; 9, Courtesy of the Palestine YMCA, Palestine TX; 10, © Christina Cutler/Palestine Herald-Press; 11, © iosphotos/ Newscom; 12, © Carlos Barria/Reuters/Landov; 13, © Dave Cruz/Reuters/Landov; 14, © Chris McGrath/Getty Images; 15, © Steve Kajihiro/CSM/Landov; 16, © AP Images; 17, © Scott Tyler/Palestine Herald-Press; 18, Courtesy of the Boys & Girls Clubs of the Twins Cities; 19, © Paul Emmel Photography; 20, © AP Images/Jim Mone; 21, © Paul Emmel Photography; 22L, © MCT/Newscom; 22R, © AP Images/Jim Mone.

Publisher: Kenn Goin
Senior Editor: Lisa Wiseman
Creative Director: Spencer Brinker
Photo Researcher: Jennifer Bright
Design: Dawn Beard Creative

Library of Congress Cataloging-in-Publication Data

Sandler, Michael.
  Adrian Peterson / by Michael Sandler.
     p. cm. — (Football heroes making a difference)
  Includes bibliographical references and index.
  ISBN-13: 978-1-936087-59-4 (library binding)
  ISBN-10: 1-936087-59-6 (library binding)
  1. Peterson, Adrian—Juvenile literature. 2. Football players—United States—Biography—
Juvenile literature. 3. Running backs (Football) —United States—Biography—Juvenile literature.
4. Minnesota Vikings (Football team)—Juvenile literature. I. Title.
  GV939.P477S26 2010
  796.332092—dc22
  [B]

                                   2009033352

For more information, write to Bearport Publishing Company, Inc., 101 Fifth Avenue, Suite 6R, New York, New York 10003. Printed in the United States of America in North Mankato, Minnesota.

122009
090309CGE

10 9 8 7 6 5 4 3 2 1

CONTENTS

Breaking Away

Early in the second half of the game, Adrian Peterson took the **handoff**. The Minnesota Vikings' **running back** cradled the ball tightly in his arms. He burst to the left as his legs pumped up and down like the **pistons** of an engine.

Two San Diego Chargers tried to grab him, but Adrian broke away. As the Chargers looked on, he sprinted down the field and then crossed into the **end zone**. Touchdown!

The 64-yard (59-m) touchdown was Adrian's second of the game—a great day's work for any running back. Adrian wasn't finished, however. There was much, much more to come.

Adrian during the game against the Chargers on November 4, 2007

Adrian scoring a touchdown during the game against the Chargers

The 64-yard (59-m) touchdown was Adrian's seventh NFL play of 50 yards (46 m) or more, a Minnesota Vikings record. It tied the game, 14-14.

Making History

As the second half went on, Adrian kept running the ball. The yards piled up: 5 yards (5 m), 10 yards (9 m), 20 yards (18 m), and then a 46-yard (42-m) touchdown! Adrian's **rushing** had put the Vikings in position to score again and again. They built a big lead and then won the game, 35-17.

Of all the **carries** Adrian made, his last was the most special. The run was just three yards (3 m), but it sent him into the record books. During the game, Adrian had rushed for a total of 296 yards (271 m). It was the most yards in a game by any running back in NFL history.

Adrian carried the ball 30 times and scored three touchdowns in the record-breaking game.

Breaking the record was amazing enough. Even more incredible was the fact that Adrian was only a **rookie**. He had broken the record in just his ninth NFL game! **Hall of Famers** such as Walter Payton, Barry Sanders, and Eric Dickerson had never rushed for that many yards in a single game during their long careers.

Adrian avoids being tackled by San Diego Chargers linebacker Carlos Polk.

All-Day Adrian

What did Adrian do the day after setting the record? He went straight to the gym to lift 300-pound (136-kg) weights. All work, all day long—that's how Adrian likes to do things. It's also why his dad gave him the nickname—A.D. (All Day). "He called me that because I could go all day," said Adrian.

Even as a young child, Adrian never stopped running around and exercising. By the time he was seven or eight years old, he was following his father to workouts at the local YMCA. He even invented exercises for himself, like filling jugs with sand, tying them to a rope, and then racing around as fast as he could while dragging the jugs behind him

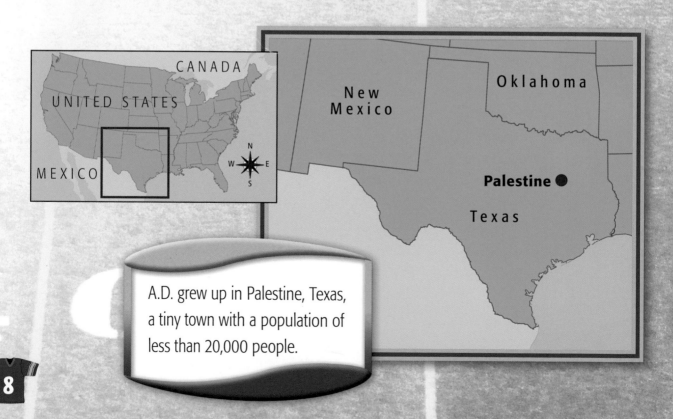

A.D. grew up in Palestine, Texas, a tiny town with a population of less than 20,000 people.

When he was a kid, Adrian would lift weights with his dad at the YMCA in Palestine.

The Country's Best

Adrian's love for exercise was matched by his love for football. As a kid, the sport came naturally to him. Even in **Pop Warner** games, his long, breathtaking runs drew "oohs" and "aahs" from coaches and parents.

Everyone in Adrian's hometown who saw him play knew that he would be a star. Adrian proved them right in his very first high school game. He rushed for a whopping 212 yards (194 m). He went on to top that in his second game with 340 yards (311 m).

By his senior year, the talented rusher was considered the top-ranked football player in the entire country. Every big college football team wanted Adrian to come and play for them.

In 2003, Adrian won the Hall Trophy, which is given each year to the country's best high school football player.

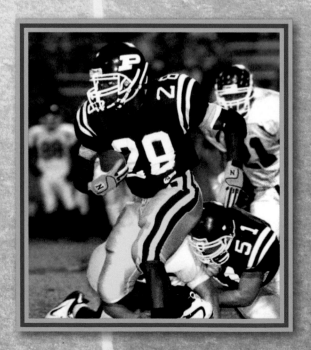

Adrian comes from a family of athletes. His mother, Bonita Jackson, was a champion high school **sprinter**. His father, Nelson Peterson, had been a college basketball star. His uncle, Ivory Lee Brown, was an NFL player.

Adrian also ran track while he was in high school.

Choosing Oklahoma

In 2004, after visiting many schools, Adrian decided to go to the University of Oklahoma. Why? He loved how hard the players on the team worked during practice. "To see the training they were going through. . . I knew that if I went there," said A.D., "I wouldn't be cheating myself."

At Oklahoma, Adrian plunged right into practice. On summer days with the sun scorching down on him, he ran one sprint after another. At the gym, he spent hours pumping weights, strengthening his arms and legs.

On opening day of his **freshman season**, A.D. showed what hard work could do. He carried the ball 16 times for exactly 100 yards (91 m).

A.D. was the first Oklahoma freshman to begin with a 100-yard (91-m) game in 35 years.

Adrian scores for Oklahoma during the 2007 Fiesta Bowl.

A.D. went on to rush for 1,925 yards (1,760 m) during the 2004 season, an **NCAA** freshman record. His outstanding play helped his team, the Sooners, to a perfect 12-0 regular season record. Over the next two years, he became known as a fearsome and fearless running back willing to do anything to gain an extra yard.

New Star in Minnesota

In 2007, after three years at Oklahoma, Adrian entered the NFL **draft**. The Minnesota Vikings picked him, making him the first running back chosen. A.D. quickly made his coaches happy with their choice. He opened his rookie year with one great performance after another—including his amazing 296-yard (271-m) record-breaking game.

In all, Adrian gained 1,341 yards (1,226 m) in 2007 and scored 12 touchdowns. He was named NFL **Offensive** Rookie of the Year and was chosen for the **Pro Bowl**. Most rookies would be satisfied with just making the Pro Bowl. Not A.D.—he wanted to star in it. Against the league's best players, he took the Pro Bowl by storm—running for 129 yards (118 m).

Adrian holding up a Vikings jersey on draft day in 2007

Adrian with his MVP trophy
after the Pro Bowl

Adrian was named MVP—most
valuable player—of the Pro Bowl.

In a Hurry

Adrian became an NFL star in just a few games. He began using his success to help others just as quickly. As soon as he put on a Vikings uniform, A.D. began brainstorming ways to give something back to the people of Palestine.

Adrian was always very grateful for the support his hometown had given him. It had helped him grow as an athlete and achieve NFL success. He wanted to give the same support to other Palestine kids. So after his rookie season, when he started a summer football camp in Oklahoma, he made sure to fly 20 kids who lived in Palestine to the camp.

Adrian avoids a tackle by a young athlete during his annual football camp.

Adrian hands out boxes of food and personal items to families in Palestine.

Adrian also wanted to help families from his hometown who were struggling to make ends meet. In June 2009, for example, Adrian and a group called Feed the Children gave out 25,000 pounds (11,340 kg) of food and other goods to 400 Palestine families.

Local Helper

Adrian also began working with two groups in Minnesota that are very important to him personally. One is the Boys & Girls Clubs of America, a group that runs art, education, and athletic programs that help teach kids the skills they need to succeed in life. Adrian knows just how valuable these programs are. He spent many afternoons taking part in them while growing up in Texas.

The second group Adrian works with is the Special Olympics, which gives people with **disabilities** the chance to compete in sports. Adrian works out with Special Olympics athletes and helps raise money for the group. The cause is close to his heart. "I have cousins with disabilities, and I'm sure everybody has someone in their family that has some type of disability," says Adrian.

Adrian poses for a photo with some children from the Boys & Girls Clubs of the Twin Cities.

Adrian (far left) works with young athletes from the Special Olympics Minnesota during a Punt, Pass, and Kick clinic.

For the last two years, Adrian has hosted a Punt, Pass, and Kick **clinic** for 50 Special Olympics kids. The children get to learn skills and throw around footballs with Adrian.

Already a Hero

Adrian followed up his **phenomenal** rookie year with an equally amazing 2008–2009 season. His team won the NFC North **division** title and made it into the playoffs. A.D.'s 1,760 rushing yards (1,609 m) were key to Minnesota's success.

It's almost hard to imagine how good Adrian can become. With his talent, the Hall of Fame is within reach. Even his biggest dream—to become the greatest football player ever—seems possible.

Yet Adrian doesn't have to wait to become a hero. He already is one to his fans, to the people of Palestine, Texas, and to the kids he hopes to continue to inspire with his success. "I always wanted to be in a position to be able to give back to the community," says Adrian. "It feels good that I'm able to reach out and inspire the young kids."

Adrian at training camp before the 2009–2010 season

Adrian poses with some athletes from the Special Olympics Minnesota on May 27, 2008.

In addition to the Boys & Girls Clubs and the Special Olympics, Adrian works with other groups such as the African American Adoption Agency and the Make-A-Wish **Foundation**.

The Adrian File

Adrian is a hero both on and off the field. Here are some of the highlights.

In the spring after his rookie season, Adrian started an organization to help him achieve his goal of building a better future for kids. It's called the All Day Foundation, and it holds special events to raise money for all the groups that Adrian supports.

By rushing 129 yards (118 m) in the 2008 Pro Bowl, Adrian achieved the second-highest rushing total in the history of this all-star game.

Only five running backs in NFL history have gained more than 3,000 yards (2,743 m) in their first two seasons. Adrian is one of them, along with Eric Dickerson, Edgerrin James, Clinton Portis, and Earl Campbell.

In each of Adrian's first two seasons, he led the league in rushing yards per game.

Glossary

carries (KA-reez) rushing attempts; turns taken running with the football

clinic (KLIN-ik) a place where people can go to practice their football skills and learn more about the sport

disabilities (*diss*-uh-BILL-uh-teez) conditions that make it hard for people to go about their daily activities

division (di-VIZH-uhn) teams that are grouped together in the NFL and compete against one another for a playoff spot

draft (DRAFT) an event in which professional teams take turns choosing college players to play for them

end zone (END ZOHN) the area at either end of a football field where touchdowns are scored

foundation (foun-DAY-shuhn) an organization that supports or gives money to worthwhile causes

freshman season (FRESH-muhn SEE-zuhn) the part of a person's first year of high school or college when a sport is played

Hall of Famers (HAWL UHV FAYM-urz) the very best football players ever to play the sport; athletes chosen to be in the Hall of Fame

handoff (HAND-awf) a play in which the quarterback hands the football to another player

NCAA (EN-SEE-AYE-AYE) National Collegiate Athletic Association; a group that runs college sports

offensive (aw-FEN-siv) a kind of player whose job it is to score points

phenomenal (fuh-NOM-uh-nuhl) amazing, incredible

pistons (PISS-tuhnz) metal parts inside an engine that slide up and down quickly and forcefully

Pop Warner (POP WORN-ur) a group that runs football leagues and programs for kids

Pro Bowl (PROH BOHL) the yearly all-star game for the season's best NFL players

rookie (RUK-ee) a first-year player

running back (RUHN-ing BAK) a player whose job it is to run with the football

rushing (RUHSH-ing) running with the football

sprinter (SPRINT-ur) a person who runs short, fast races

Bibliography

Evans, Thayer. "The Pride of Palestine: Texas Town Follows its Star." *The New York Times* (September 23, 2007).

Wuebben, Joe. "Run Adrian Run." *Muscle & Fitness* (October 2008).

The Palestine Herald-Press

The Pioneer Press (St. Paul)

Read More

Currie, Stephen. *Adrian Peterson.* Broomall, PA: Mason Crest (2009).

LeBoutillier, Nate. *The Story of the Minnesota Vikings.* Mankato, MN: Creative Education (2009).

Stewart, Mark. *The Minnesota Vikings.* Chicago: Norwood House (2009).

Learn More Online

To learn more about Adrian Peterson, the Minnesota Vikings, and the All Day Foundation, visit **www.bearportpublishing.com/FootballHeroes**

Index